Dedication

To Moralee, my wife:
Whose presence in my life
stirs the creative and romantic
juices inside me,
which manifest themselves
in a desire to love her
through the meals I create for her.

Published by CatsCurious Press
First Edition, 2007

Copyright © 2006 Carl R. Wendtland
Illustrations Copyright © 2007 Lanny Liu
Photographs Copyright © 2007 Sonya M. Shannon
Wine Selection 101 Copyright © 2007 Dr. John Chamberlin

All Rights Reserved.
No Part of this book may be used or reproduced in any manner whatsoever without written permission except in the case of brief quotations embodied in critical articles and reviews.

For information, address:
Book Editor
CatsCurious Press
5312 Dillon Circle
Fort Worth, TX 76137

Library of Congress Control Number: 2007928404

ISBN 0-9790889-1-7
ISBN-13 978-0-9790889-1-9

COOKING YOUR WAY TO
Romance

By Carl R. Wendtland

Illustrations by Lanny Liu

Acknowledgements

Thanks to my good friend, Dr. John Chamberlin, for the appendix on 'Wine Selection 101'. John's knowledge of wine is legendary in our circle. I am pleased and honored he consented to share his unique insight as a contribution to my book. Pay close attention to what he has to say, and remember that the knowledge he imparts will be a key factor in the success of your quest in 'cooking your way to romance'.

Thanks to my good friend and kindred cooking spirit, Bill Tennison, for the wonderful Guacamole dip recipe. It truly is the best I've sampled through the years. Bill and I share an enthusiasm for creating exciting meals at home.

TABLE OF *Contents*

Introduction	7
In the beginning, there was chicken	9
A little bit of Italy	13
From the grill to the table	21
Lunch is served	27
How's them Enchiladas?	33
Mort Canard	39
The Big Easy	47
Oh La La Lasagna	53
Notes from the Range	59

MORE COOKING YOUR WAY TO *Romance*   60

Seafood with La Salsa de Carlos	61
Carl's Pork de La Valle	63
Chicken Scaloppini	65
Coquilles St Jacques	67
Spanish Cannelloni	68
Spicy Chicken (or Shrimp) Salad	70
Chicken & Broccoli Pizza	71

Appendix A: Wine Selection 101	73
Appendix B: Setting the Table	78
Appendix C: Metric Conversions	80
Glossary of Terms	81

A Note from the *Editor*

Carl has taken the time to write the recipes in this cookbook in a clear and simple language, making them as easy to follow as possible.

Seasoned veterans may find the directions unorthodox, but when followed properly, an inexperienced cook should meet with success every time.

Introduction

Good looks, a nice car and a promising career! What else does a man need to attract or rekindle the interest of the woman of his dreams? After all, what else could a woman want, right?

How about a man who isn't too full of himself for starters... a man who will value a woman above his image, his career, and his friends? How would he convey an idea like that?

It can be summed up in one word: "Romance".

But how does he go about creating this essential ingredient? What if he lacks the self-confidence of other men, those smooth-talkers who have all the lines?

Well my friend, here's the answer: Women *love* a man who can cook. You can't cook? No worries, that's where I come in! I have intended this little book to be a 'handbook' to help you succeed where others have failed. I've written it in a way that will pique your interest and plainly explains how to make the enclosed recipes so that you will have no questions or doubts. I can put you on a path to becoming the object of her desires *and* a coveted commodity in the eyes of the women in your universe. Yes, you will have to learn to follow directions (I know it's not in the natural order of things for a man to follow directions) but believe me, it will be worth your while!

Warning: This journey is not for the weak... It will take a real man -- because *real men aren't afraid to cook.*

So if you think you can handle it and you're ready to be desired by women, then turn the page and read on!

I appreciate your intentions, but who's going to clean up this mess when you're through?

IN THE BEGINNING,
THERE WAS Chicken

In the beginning I had no idea what I was doing or where it would lead me. I took that first step for selfish reasons actually; little did I know that it would be the beginning of my transformation from a self-centered schmuck, to a true romantic.

It was some time in the 70's, about 1976 I think. I came home one evening, and as I entered the kitchen, I asked my wife "What's for dinner?"

"Chicken," she answered.

"Chicken! I don't want chicken tonight, I want veal parmigiana."

"Too bad," she said, "we have no veal, so we're having chicken."

Most nights I would have let it go at that, but for some reason this night was different. I guess I must have been feeling a little amorous and wanted the sort of meal that would kick-start the evening into a romantic direction.

I thought about it for a moment and an idea came to me. "We *are* having parmigiana tonight, chicken parmigiana!" I wasn't sure if it would actually work (after all, my wife was the cook, not me!) but I dove in anyway. She gladly consented to let me take over.

First, I skinned the chicken, and then carefully cut all the meat off of the bones. *Hmm, still looks like chicken*, I thought. "Where is the meat hammer?" I asked aloud.

"In the left-hand drawer" she said.

I got it out, plopped a piece of chicken onto the cutting board in front of me, and then proceeded to pound the meat flat. This was working -- but I made an awful mess! Little pieces of chicken flew all over the kitchen, sticking like glue to the cabinets, the walls, and the floor. But on the counter in front of me was a wide, flat piece of meat. *Yes!* I thought, *that looks like veal!*

I looked through our cookbooks and found the recipe for parmigiana. I followed the directions, substituting the chicken for veal. (I found real satisfaction in cooking that first meal. The creativity I'd shown impressed my wife, and the meal astounded her.)

"This tastes like veal!" she exclaimed.

 (Or somewhere between chicken and veal anyway, and a lot cheaper than veal too!)

The experience had the desired effect -- she had started the evening amused with my efforts but ended up showing her appreciation in a very romantic way. I felt quite proud of myself and found that I really liked her reaction. I knew that I had stumbled onto something here, and was eager to explore the relationship between cooking and romance further.

It's 2007 now; I have evolved into the primary cook in our house, mostly because I really enjoy it. I have developed a reputation I endeavor to maintain (women talk at work you know), so my efforts have become known. Over the years, I continued to look for other special meals that I could prepare and became interested in creating a romantic atmosphere at the table, as well. Our theme nights centered on ethnic dishes are envied far and wide. Women have actually asked my wife if they could borrow me! (she has always pleasantly refused. I wonder if she's afraid they won't return me?)

But now, it's your turn, if you dare! Just remember these three basic rules, and you will never fail:

You are doing this for her.
You are doing this for her.
You are doing this for her.

That's right, to be a true romantic and to be desired by the woman you love, you have to truly do it *for her*. If you're doing it for yourself, she'll know.

And in the end, you'll fail.

In this era of personal fulfillment and self-gratification, if you can learn to put the needs and desires of the person you love before your own, you will be miles ahead of your competition in the relationship department. You will truly be on your way to a lasting and fulfilling lifetime partnership.

Wow! this meal really sings to me, but I still want to know who's cleaning the kitchen…

A LITTLE BIT OF *Italy*

Congratulations, you've taken the first step!

I've learned a lot since that maiden meal, and I'm willing to share what I have learned with you (for instance, how to keep the little chicken pieces from flying all over the kitchen!) So let's get started.

The first thing you should do, is set your table for the evening dinner. You can look up how to do this in Appendix B at the end of this book. Doing this ahead of time allows you to concentrate on creating the perfect atmosphere for the evening without distracting you from cooking later (and possibly ruining one of your dishes). Remember the tablecloth, cloth napkins, candlelight, and of course selecting the appropriate music to enhance the destination you intend to portray. Also remember to select and chill (if needed) an appropriate wine or beverage; you can find a list of those in Appendix A. Selecting what you plan to wear ahead of time is also a good idea.

Now you are ready to concentrate on the creation of your soon-to-be-discovered mystique! I started with chicken and it worked for me, so roll up your sleeves and don't be a 'chicken'. Let's cook up a little bit of Italy for her!

Menu:
Chicken Parmigiana
Parmesan Baked Potatoes
Tossed Salad

CHICKEN *Parmigiana*

The Sauce
1- 15 oz can of stewed or diced tomatoes Italian style
1 tsp of oregano
Pepper to taste
1 tsp of basil
1/8 tsp of garlic

The Meat
Two chicken breasts
One egg, lightly beaten
1/3 cup of grated Parmesan cheese
1 small onion, thinly sliced
12 saltine crackers
2 to 4 tbsp of olive oil
1 tbsp of parsley

The Rest
Splash of vermouth
1 cup (4 oz) sliced or shredded mozzarella cheese

Things you will need
2 shallow bowls (I use pie plates)
1 large zipper-style plastic bag
1 small zipper-style plastic bag
Some plastic wrap
1 medium frying pan
1 small pan
1 baking dish (9"x13" or smaller)
1 flat-sided meat hammer
1 rolling pin (optional, you can use the meat hammer instead)

Open the can of stewed tomatoes and puree (blend until smooth) with a mixer. Add the oregano, basil, garlic, and pepper to the tomato puree. Place in a small pan, bring to a boil, reduce the heat to low and simmer (cook slowly on a *very low* boil) while stirring occasionally.

Okay, now put the 12-saltine crackers in the small zipper-style plastic bag (don't forget to seal it). Use the rolling pin to roll over the bag and crush the crackers. If you do not have a rolling pin, then carefully use the *flat side* of the meat hammer to crush the crackers. Now open the bag and add the Parmesan cheese and the tablespoon of parsley to the cracker crumbs.

Close the bag and mix the two together, then pour this mixture into one of the pie plates. Crack the egg into the other pie plate and lightly beat it (scramble) with a fork.

Take the large zipper-style plastic bag and put one of the thawed chicken breasts into it. Get all the excess air out and seal the bag. Carefully pound the chicken with the flat side of the meat hammer about five times. Don't hit it too hard or you will break the chicken apart. Now turn it over and hit the other side another five times (carefully!). With practice you will learn how much force to use. You should now have a much flatter and wider piece of meat. Take this piece out of the bag set it aside, and place the other breast in the bag and repeat.

Now dip the flattened chicken fillets into the beaten egg. Remember to turn them over and coat both sides, then dip them in the cracker crumb/parmesan cheese mixture. Again, coat both sides well. Heat 2 tablespoons of olive oil in the medium frying pan. When hot, place one of the fillets in the pan and cook until browned. You are looking for a golden color. If you leave it in too long it will burn, so be careful. Turn the fillet over and brown the other side. When done, place the fillet in the 9"x13" baking dish. Before you brown the other fillet you may need to add

2 more tablespoons of olive oil to the pan. When both are done and in the baking dish, squirt a splash of the dry vermouth in the frying pan before you turn off the burner. Swirl this around to capture the cracker crumbs/ parmesan cheese residue in the pan and then pour it over the fillets.

Next, slice the onion thinly and place the slices on top the two chicken fillets. Sprinkle the shredded mozzarella cheese over each fillet. Finally, pour the tomato puree you've been simmering on the stove over the two fillets (don't forget to turn off the stove burner). Cover the baking dish with plastic wrap and place it in the refrigerator for now.

Got all that? Okay! Now let's make the potatoes.

PARMESAN BAKED *Potatoes*

The Potatoes
2 large potatoes
¼ cup of grated Parmesan cheese
1/3 cup of sour cream
3 tbsp of butter
1 tbsp of Parsley
A sprinkle of Paprika

Things you will need
A potato peeler
A steamer pan (this a pan that has a basket in it and a lid.)
A potato masher or electric mixer
A small baking dish

Peel the potatoes, rinse them off under the faucet, and then cut the potatoes into small pieces and place them in the steamer basket. Put about 1 inch of water in the bottom of the pan, insert the basket in it and cover the basket/pan with the lid. Place the pan on the stove and heat on high. Check periodically by poking the potatoes with a fork. When they are tender, turn off burner and remove them from the stove. Drain the remaining water from pan; pour the potatoes from the basket into the pan. Mash the potatoes (or blend with the electric mixer) and then add the parmesan cheese, sour cream, butter, and the parsley. Mash or blend again until smooth. Scoop the potato mixture into the baking dish and sprinkle with paprika.

Now, preheat the oven to 350 degrees and place the potatoes and the chicken parmigiana in (don't forget to remove the plastic wrap!). Set the oven timer to 35 minutes. While these dishes are cooking, make the salad (page 18). When the timer goes off, serve the chicken and potatoes hot with your fresh tossed salad on the side.

TOSSED *Salad*

The Salad
Romaine lettuce
Tomatoes
Fresh mushrooms
Black olives
Red onions
Grated cheese
Dried bread croutons
Bacon bits

First, rinse the lettuce in the sink. Shake to dry, and place on a cutting board. I like to cut the lettuce into thin strips, but you can cut it to suit your own preference. Slice or chop your remaining ingredients and toss them with the lettuce. I like to serve salad in individual salad bowls so I usually have several choices of dressing available. A nice artistic twist is to arrange a few tomatoes or other ingredients in the salad to suggest a floral design. Another suggestion is buy yourself a hand held cheese grater, and grate some parmesan cheese on the salad at the table, just as they do at fine restaurants.

There are many wonderful things you can put in a salad. Listed above are some of my favorites, but don't be afraid to substitute some of your own.

This guy gets cuter every meal he cooks for me!

FROM THE GRILL TO THE *Table*

Well, how did it go? I'll bet you surprised her and left her at least a little bit intrigued.

Alright, so maybe she didn't reward you in a romantic way after your first meal. Don't feel bad just because mine did (after all, she was already my wife!). Did you remember to set a nice table? How about candlelight and a nice white wine? Maybe you forgot the importance of cloth napkins or soft romantic dinner music. Remember, "Romance" is the name of the game! Either way, I bet she is looking at you in a slightly different light, so let's try again.

Do you like to grill out? Here's a fairly easy but impressive recipe when presented correctly. This will give you a chance to hone your 'atmosphere' creating skills, while not taxing your culinary skills too much. Remember your pre-dinner drill before you get started -- table set, beverage and atmosphere (especially with a dinner like this!). It goes right from the grill to the table.

Oh, and with this one, you'll have to be dressed for dinner before you start.

Menu:
Grilled Salmon over Salad
French Bread with Butter

GRILLED SALMON OVER *Salad*

The Salmon
2 salmon fillets
Olive oil
Lemon/pepper seasoning

The Dijon Butter
2 tbsp of soft butter
1 tbsp of Dijon mustard
½ tsp of tarragon

The Salad
Leaf lettuce (I prefer red leaf lettuce)
½ cup cherry tomatoes
½ cup mandarin oranges (found in the canned fruit aisle of your grocery store)
½ cup fresh mushrooms (sliced)
1/8 cup sliced black olives
1/8 cup of sweetened dried cranberries
1/8 cup of walnuts
Raspberry and walnut vinaigrette dressing

The Bread
1 loaf of French bread, sliced
Soft butter to spread on the French Bread

Things you will need
A grill, of course (charcoal or gas)
Grill tools (spatula and/or tongs)

Make a 'Dijon Butter' by mixing the soft butter with the Dijon mustard and the tarragon. Once thoroughly mixed, set it aside.

Cut or tear the leaf lettuce (not too small this time) and place on two dinner plates. Add the mandarin orange slices, the cherry tomatoes, the fresh mushrooms, the black olives, the dried cranberries, and the walnuts to the lettuce. Splash some of the raspberry and walnut vinaigrette on the salads and set the plates in the refrigerator for now (this should not be done more than an hour in advance or else the lettuce may get soggy).

Brush the salmon fillets with some olive oil on both sides then lightly dust them with the lemon/pepper seasoning. Place them on a *very hot* grill for about 2 ½ to 3 minutes per side. Be careful when turning in case they stick. Lay the fillets over the salads and brush them with the Dijon Butter.

Serve immediately with a basket of French bread and butter.

I sat right here and watched him prepare this, but I'd swear he ordered this in from a classy restaurant.

LUNCH IS *Served*

Nice little dish, hey? My wife argued for years that she disliked salmon, and didn't want to try it again. This one turned out to be a win/win situation! I won the argument and she let me cook it for her. She won because she agreed it was wonderful, and looked forward to having it again. It turns out she had only had canned salmon in the past. She loved the fact that it was such a light meal. No heavy carbs to worry about.

By now, your lady is realizing that there just might be a bit more to you than your good looks and stable career. She is beginning to wonder if you will invite her back, and actually know more than two dishes to cook. (Oh, by the way, she really liked the light dish as well didn't she?) Let's take things down a notch, and show her that you're sincere and can do more than dinner. Afternoons can be romantic, right? Let's go back to Italy and do lunch.

Huddle up; remember the pre-dinner drill (in this case luncheon drill). Prepare your salads first and place them in the refrigerator. You've made them before, so no need to bore you with instructions on that again.

Menu
Carmora's Tuscan Style Soup
Italian bread sticks
Tossed Salad

CARMORA'S TUSCAN STYLE *Soup*

The Soup
2 large red potatoes
1 small red potato
1 tsp of dried minced garlic
1 cup of milk
2 chicken bouillon cubes
2 cups of water
½ tsp of salt
2 oz of Monterey jack cheese
2 tbsp of minced parsley (fresh if possible)
1 tsp of minced onion
¼ tsp of pepper
2 tbsp of butter
1/3 cup of ground Italian sausage
A few leaves of leaf lettuce
Some Parmesan cheese (grated or block)

The Bread
Your favorite store-bought breadsticks, prepared as directed

Tossed Salad
See page 18

Things you will need
1 medium pot
Potato masher or electric mixer
1 small frying pan
A hand held cheese grater (if you use block parmesan)

In the small frying pan, brown the Italian sausage, remove from heat and set aside.

Now peel and rinse off the 2 large red potatoes. Cut them into small cube shaped pieces. Put them into the medium pot along with the water, chicken bullion cubes, onion, garlic, salt, and pepper. Bring this to a boil over a high heat. Then reduce heat to low, cover the pot and simmer about 15 to 20 minutes. Remember to stir occasionally.

When the time is up, remove the soup mixture from the stove and mash or mix the potato cubes into the liquid until smooth. Next add the milk, Monterey jack cheese, butter, parsley, and Italian sausage to the pot. Return the pot to the stove and heat on medium, stirring until the cheese is melted.

Now wash off the small red potato, but do not peel it. Cut the small potato into thin slices about ¼" thick, and add it to the pot. Continue cooking and stirring occasionally, until slices are tender but *not* mushy -- you want them to be somewhat firm. A caution here: If you don't watch this dish while it's cooking, it's easy to burn. Milk burns easily. Also important is to keep this soup thin. You can accomplish this by adding more milk. (You don't want to be forced into calling an audible this late in the game!)

Your lady is probably already on her way over, and as anxious as she probably is for this next dining experience you don't want to be sacked for a loss. Now you need to multi-task here a bit (most women think we men can't do this). I know it's only two things and not much of a scramble for a quarterback like you, but trust me you need the practice for later on in the game. So while cooking and stirring in the potato slices, you'll need to heat the oven up to 200° F. and warm up the Italian bread sticks.

When the breadsticks are warm, and the soup is ready, put the salads on the table, fill the soup bowls, cut some ribbons of fresh lettuce and place them in the soup as a garnish. Put the soup and bread sticks on the table. Invite your lady to be seated. Grate some Parmesan cheese over the soups, sit down and enjoy.

❉   ❉   ❉

This is a recipe that my wife and I worked on together actually. We used to order something similar at one of our favorite restaurants. We enjoyed it so much, we decided to work on our own version to prepare at home. It took us several tries, but we finally ended up with a dish we were both very happy with. We now can enjoy it in a more intimate and romantic setting… One of our own making!

This guy's imagination drives me wild, and so does his dancing!

HOW'S THEM *Enchiladas?*

Wow! She now knows you can make soup from scratch as well. She is impressed. You might have noticed other women looking at you lately. The word is starting to get out. "He cooks for you? Wow! I wish my man would do that." Remember, women talk to each other.

By now you're no longer worrying over each meal. Your confidence level is on the rise, and I hope you're really starting to enjoy treating her to your culinary endeavors. At this point you might be wondering who is looking forward more to your next meal, you or your lady?

Mexico is nice this time of year. Heck, Mexico is nice any time of the year! Let's travel south of the border. Are you ready for your first theme night? Before you get started on this one, remember that atmosphere is important here: décor, lighting, music, proper attire. That's right! Dress for the occasion, and don't forget the cervesa or sangria either.

How's them Enchiladas?

Menu
Chicken Enchiladas with Verde sauce
Rice and Frijoles
Chips & Guacamole (or Salsa, your choice. To be placed on the table before dinner.)

CHICKEN *Enchiladas*
WITH VERDE SAUCE

The Enchiladas
2 chicken breast fillets
5 oz of shredded Monterey jack cheese
6 corn tortillas

The Verde Sauce
1 small onion chopped
1 tsp of minced garlic
4 sprigs of cilantro
½ of a 7 oz can of jalapeño peppers
1- 26 oz can of crushed tomatillos (or whole tomatillos, drained)

The Rest
2 cups of Minute rice
1- 15 oz can of Mexican style chili beans

Things you will need
2 medium sized frying pans
4 *oven safe* dinner plates (oval if possible)
1 medium sized steamer pot with lid.
2 small bowls
Hand held blender
1 medium size pot with lid
1 small plate (to use as a lid for one of the small bows)

First, open the can of tomatillos (and drain and purée them if using whole), and pour the rest into one of the two frying pans. Next, open the can of jalapeño peppers, drain off the juice, and puree them with a hand held blender; pour this into the tomatillos. Add the chopped onion, cilantro, and the minced garlic, then place the pan on the stove over a medium heat. When the tomatillo mixture starts to boil, reduce theheat and simmer, stirring occasionally.

Next, place about an inch of water in the steamer pot, place the steamer basket over it, put the chicken in the basket and put the lid on the top. Put this on the stove over a high heat. Check the chicken periodically. When it can easily be pulled apart with two forks, remove the steamer pot from heat and use the two forks to shred the chicken. Put the shredded chicken into one of the small bowls and add about a 1 oz of shredded Monterey jack cheese, and about ¼ cup of the tomatillo sauce that you are simmering. Mix this well and then cover the bowl with a small plate for now (to keep the meat moist). Clean off the hand held blender, as you will need it again.

Open the can of Mexican chili beans and pour it into the other small bowl. Puree the beans with the hand held blender. Set this aside.

Cook the rice in the medium pot according to directions on the package. When done, leave covered and set aside.

Now put 2 tbsp of oil in the other frying pan, and heat on medium. When hot, lay a corn tortilla in the pan. Cook the tortilla until it starts to blister or bubble, then turn it over and heat the other side. Once the other side has begin to blister and bubble as well, transfer the tortilla to the sauce, and coat both sides of it with the sauce. Lay the tortilla on one of the plates, spoon some chicken onto it and fold it in half, gently. Repeat this process, overlapping the enchiladas on the plate.

Remember that you may need to add a bit of oil to the frying pan periodically as you fry the tortillas (2 to 3 enchiladas per plate is enough). Ladle a serving of rice and a serving of beans on each plate. Pour the remaining sauce over the enchiladas, rice and beans. Top all with the remaining shredded cheese. Place the plates into the oven (preheated to 350 degrees) for about 20 minutes. Remove from the oven and place the hot plate on top of another plate (a cool one), and serve.

BILL'S *Guacamole Dip*

Bill's Guacamole Dip (for two)

The Guacamole
1 avocado
1 tbsp onion (finely chopped)
1½ tbsp tomato (finely chopped)
1 tbsp red bell pepper (finely chopped)
1 tbsp cilantro (finely chopped)
½ tsp jalapeno pepper (finely chopped)
¼ tsp fresh crushed garlic
¼ tsp of hot sauce
¾ tsp lime juice

Tortilla chips

Cut around the avocado lengthwise to the stone (avocado pit). Twist the two halves to separate and take out the stone. With knife, cut avocado meat in a crosshatch pattern and then dig the meat out with a spoon. Place the avocado meat in a small bowl and mash with a fork. Add all the other ingredients and mix well with the fork. Place dip in a small serving dish and serve with tortilla chips.

For a time, we lived in Corpus Christi, TX. We both really enjoyed good Mexican food and the authentic feel of the many fine restaurants in this beautiful city. We've since returned North but miss the food! We have not again found a restaurant that could provide the flavor or the atmosphere we missed, so I've attempted to recreate it myself, at home. My wife looks forward to enjoying our Mexican theme nights. People might think we're a bit eccentric (if they saw us singing and dancing to the music) but they would really enjoy my enchiladas!

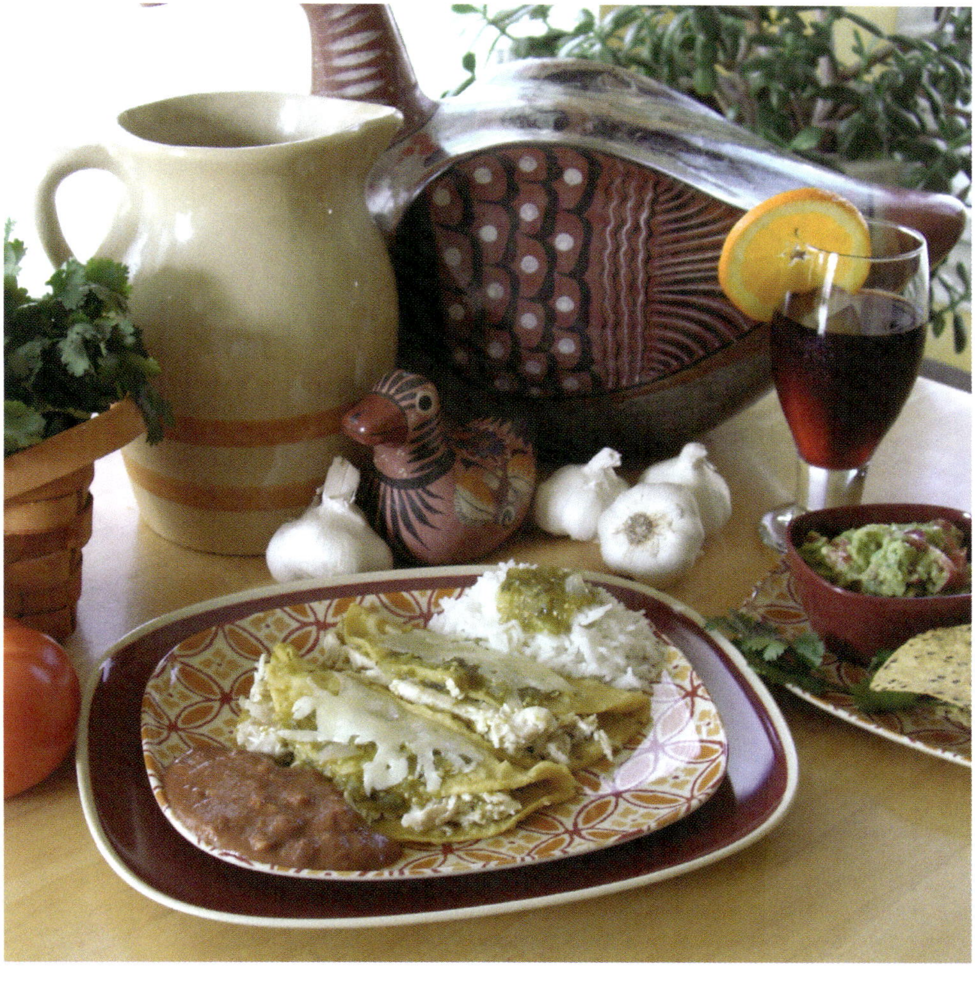

A duck! If he can pull this one off, this guy's mine! I'm going straight to the assayer's office to stake my claim. He's pure gold!

MORT *Canard*

Well, how'd it go? You know a woman likes a man who is cultured and well traveled. That's one of the things we plan to achieve here you know. So far we've had you cooking your way to Italy and Mexico, and doing a little grilling. Before we're done you will treat her to other exotic places as well. It doesn't really matter that you've never actually been to some of these places. Through romantically designed and prepared meals, she'll feel that you were taking her there for the evening. You see, we're not just cooking a meal here -- we're creating an event for her to remember, one that she'll still be thinking and talking about Monday morning. I imagine the conversation going something like this:

❋ ❋ ❋

"What did you do last weekend Jane?"

"Oh, my Bill invited me over for dinner. It was so romantic! He made chicken enchiladas with verde sauce. He knows how much I love Mexican food. It was delicious, and the atmosphere, wow! Soft authentic music in the background, candlelight, and the table appeared as if straight from a cantina. We even dressed for the occasion. I'm telling you he thought of everything, even my favorite Mexican beer. How was your weekend?"

"Well, not as good as yours. Frank took me to a ball game and then out for pizza. You know how I hate baseball! It's so slow! I'd have much rather gone to Mexico with you and Bill. What are you doing next weekend? Do you want to go to a show?"

"Sorry, Bill has already invited me over again for dinner."

"Really! What exotic place is he creating for you this time?"

"France, I think. Do you want to help me find something to wear over lunch break today?"

"You lucky girl! Do you think a bit of Bill will ever wear off on Frank?"

"One can hope!"

❈   ❈   ❈

You see my friend, once she starts looking forward to the next exotic place you plan to take her, she is a "mort canard" (for those of you who don't speak French, that's a dead duck!)

No, we're really not interested in doing away with her. The French however do have many tasty ways of preparing duck. She won't turn back now; she wants and needs the next romantic escape. And that brings us to our next dinner. It's a dish I've had many times in restaurants, and have made a crusade of developing a recipe that I was satisfied with. It has become one of my personal favorites!

By now you've remembered the pre-dinner drill, so I won't bore you with that. Let's get started!

Menu
Roast Duck on a bed of White and Wild Rice
Green Beans Almondine

ROAST *Duck*
ON A BED OF WHITE & WILD RICE

The Duck
One duck (with orange sauce packet included)
One head of celery
Two large onions
One apple
One orange
Some poultry rub
A small glass of orange juice
A box of white & wild rice

Things you will need
A roasting pan with a lid
A wire roasting rack
Poultry scissors
Oven safe plates
2 small oven safe custard dishes

Preheat oven to 350 degrees, and line the bottom of the roasting pan with the Celery stalks. Then slice the two onions and place the slices on top on the celery. This will absorb the grease from the duck during cooking. Place the wire roasting rack on top of the onions (my rack has sides that raise up to hold the bird in place). Remove the orange glaze packet and all innards from the duck cavity. Rinse the duck with water inside and out. Coat the inside of the duck cavity with some orange juice, and then season it with some poultry rub. Cut the apple and orange into wedges. Place the wedges inside the cavity of the duck. Pour the rest of the glass of orange juice over the duck and season it with the poultry rub.

Put the duck on the roasting rack, breast side up, and cover. When oven is ready, bake duck for 3 ½ hours, or until golden brown and tender. Every oven is different, so time may vary. Remove duck from oven when done. Lift duck, rack and all out of the roasting pan and place on a cookie sheet. Cut open breast cavity with the poultry scissors, and remove and discard fruit as well as remains in roasting pan. Let the duck cool for about ½ hour. While the duck is cooling prepare the white and wild rice according to the directions on the box. When the duck has cooled, carefully finish cutting up the breast and through the back with the poultry scissors. You should now have two halves of duck. Place them in the refrigerator for two hours. After this time take them out again.

This next step is probably the hardest part of the whole recipe. You can now carefully take the rib cage and the backbones out. All that should remain is the wing and leg bones. Be careful not to let the duck fall apart as you do this step.

Place the rice on two oven safe plates; Lay the duck halves over the rice. Cover with plastic wrap and place back in the refrigerator for later. About 45 minutes before you want to sit down for dinner, preheat the oven to 350 degrees. Take plastic wrap off the plates, and place the plates into oven for 20 to 30 minutes. At this time also open orange sauce packet, pour into the two oven safe custard dishes and place into oven to heat as well. When finished take plates from oven and put on top of another similar plate. Add a serving of Green Beans Almondine on the side and serve. The orange sauce can be either poured over the duck or placed on the side to dip pieces of duck into.

The Green Beans Almondine
2 cups of Frozen (French cut beans)
3 tbsp of slivered almonds
1 tbsp of butter

Things You Will Need
A small frying pan
A wooden spoon

In a small frying pan, lightly brown the almond in the butter and set aside. Steam the beans until they are bright green. When ready place beans on plate and top with almonds.

❄ ❄ ❄

I had a conversation with a good friend about this dinner, and about how, in the past, the duck always turned out tough. He said that was the same problem that his wife had when she prepared duck. I invited them for dinner one night, and made this duck recipe. She took one bite and exclaimed "this is wonderful, how did you do this? It's so tender!" She asked for the recipe, and when she read it she exclaimed: "You should write a cook book. The way you explain how to prepare this meal -- a novice could follow it and be successful."

So you see Audrey, you gave me the inspiration to start this book. I thought it only fair I mention you in it.

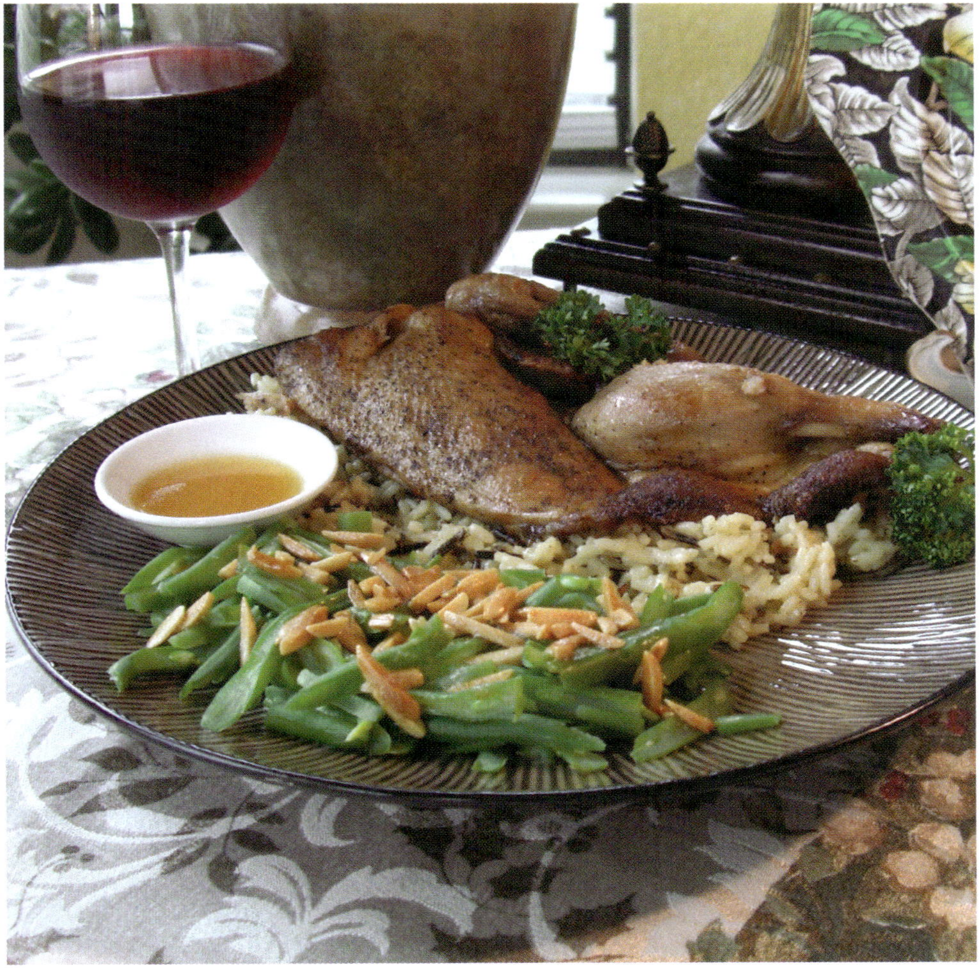

I made the right decision! I wonder what Mary's doing right now? Probably eating pizza again.

THE BIG *Easy*

Lets go to New Orleans! There is no place that I can think of in these United States that is more romantic than the "Big Easy". I know it was devastated by Hurricane Katrina, but rest assured its people are a resilient lot and they will restore it to its former glory. New Orleans is the most ethnically diverse bed of rice I've ever seen, and crawfish love it! And if crawfish love it, then I love it. You see my friend, I've never met a crawfish that I didn't like (to eat! that is).

That brings us to our next romantic dinner, Crawfish Etouff'ee! Now this dish takes a bit of time… time and attention. Don't rush this dish; good things are worth waiting for. Do not worry, it's not hard to make, only time consuming. The big plus with this dish is that you get to prove to her that it really is you that is creating all these culinary feats for her. You see, she will be there sipping a glass of wine as you prepare this one. But hey, it's not all work, you get to enjoy yourself too. I've heard it said that the time it takes to make good roux is not measured in minutes, but in beers. It takes me personally about two beers to make one.

Menu
Crawfish Etouff'ee
Corn Bread with Honey Butter (made ahead of time)
Your Favorite Salad (made ahead of time)

Prepare your cornbread and salad ahead of time so that you can eat this dish while it's hot. Any cornbread mix will do, and paired with honey-butter, is a delicious addition (see end of this section for a quick recipe for honey butter).

CRAWFISH Etouff'ee

The Etouff'ee
1 cup of butter (2 sticks)
1 cup of flower or (1/2 cup of cornstarch)
2 medium sized onions (chopped)
1 tbsp of minced garlic
1 large green bell pepper (chopped)
2 celery stalks (chopped)
1½ tbsp of tomato paste
½ tsp red pepper (cayenne)
½ tsp of ground black pepper
1- 8 oz bottle of clam juice
1 cup of chicken broth
1/3 cup of chopped fresh parsley
1 lb Package of crawfish tails
3 cups of (minute rice)
2 sprigs of fresh parsley

Don't forget your beer!

Things you will need
Seasoned cast iron Dutch oven or twelve inch skillet (<u>Cast iron is essential</u>)
A whisk
A medium sized pot with a lid
2 wide dinner bowls

The first thing you want to do is chop your onions, bell pepper, and the celery stalks, then place them in separate bowls and set aside. Make sure you have all of your ingredients handy, as they will be added to the roux in order, as you continue to stir it (keep your beer within arm's reach as well!).

Now to make the roux, take the cast iron Dutch oven or large cast iron skillet. Heat the butter on a medium heat in pan until it melts and turns clear. But **be careful not to burn it**. Then add the flour or cornstarch (which ever you prefer to use) all at once, and stir in with a whisk until smooth. If you have lumps use the backside of a wooden spoon the smooth them out. Reduce heat to 'a bit above low' and continue to stir.

Now you can open your first beer if you like, and continue to stir. Stirring is very important! If you burn the roux you will see little black or brown flecks in it and it will taste bitter and need to be discarded and started over. (Yes! you must stir continuously!) It will take about 1 hour of stirring to get the roux to be a dark peanut butter color, which is what you're looking for. An hour of conversation and sipping your beer as you stir is not too much to ask. You'll see what I mean when you sit down to enjoy this dish.

After the hour is up, it's time to add the onions, the garlic, the chopped bell pepper and the celery. Cook the mixture, stirring continuously, until the vegetables are slightly wilted and transparent. This should take about 5 minutes. Now stir in the tomato paste, cayenne pepper, and the black pepper. Then add the cup of chicken broth, the clam juice, and last but not least, the crawfish. As the sauce thickens, keep stirring. Season with a little salt, reduce heat to low, and simmer uncovered for 45 minutes, remembering to stir occasionally.

It's now time to cook the minute rice (according to the directions on the box) in the medium pot. Minute rice only takes five minutes to cook, so when it's done remove from heat and leave covered until needed. When you are done simmering the etouff'ee, stir in the fresh chopped parsley, and remove from heat.

Put a scoop of rice in the center of each dinner bowl, then, using a ladle, pour some of the Etouff'ee around the rice. Lay a sprig of fresh parsley in the center of the rice as a garnish, and serve your cornbread up in a basket or on the side. Ask your lady to be seated, serve and sit down to enjoy a wonderful meal and her admiration for creating this culinary feat for her, right before her eyes.

The Honey Butter
3 tbsp Butter, very soft (but not melted)
1 tbsp honey

Put the 3 tbsp of butter into a shallow cup and then add the 1 tbsp of honey to it. Using the back of a small spoon, smash the softened butter against the sides of the cup, incorporating the honey into it. When the butter's texture seems to have evened out, stir the mixture vigorously until its as smooth as you like. Set this off to the side to be served up with your cornbread.

❅ ❅ ❅

Wow! That is some dish, don't you think? And I've discovered that it you have a friend who has a 'gluten intolerance', you can make the roux with cornstarch instead of flour. Just use one half the amount called for, i.e. ½ cup of cornstarch for 1 cup of flour. It tastes just as wonderful!

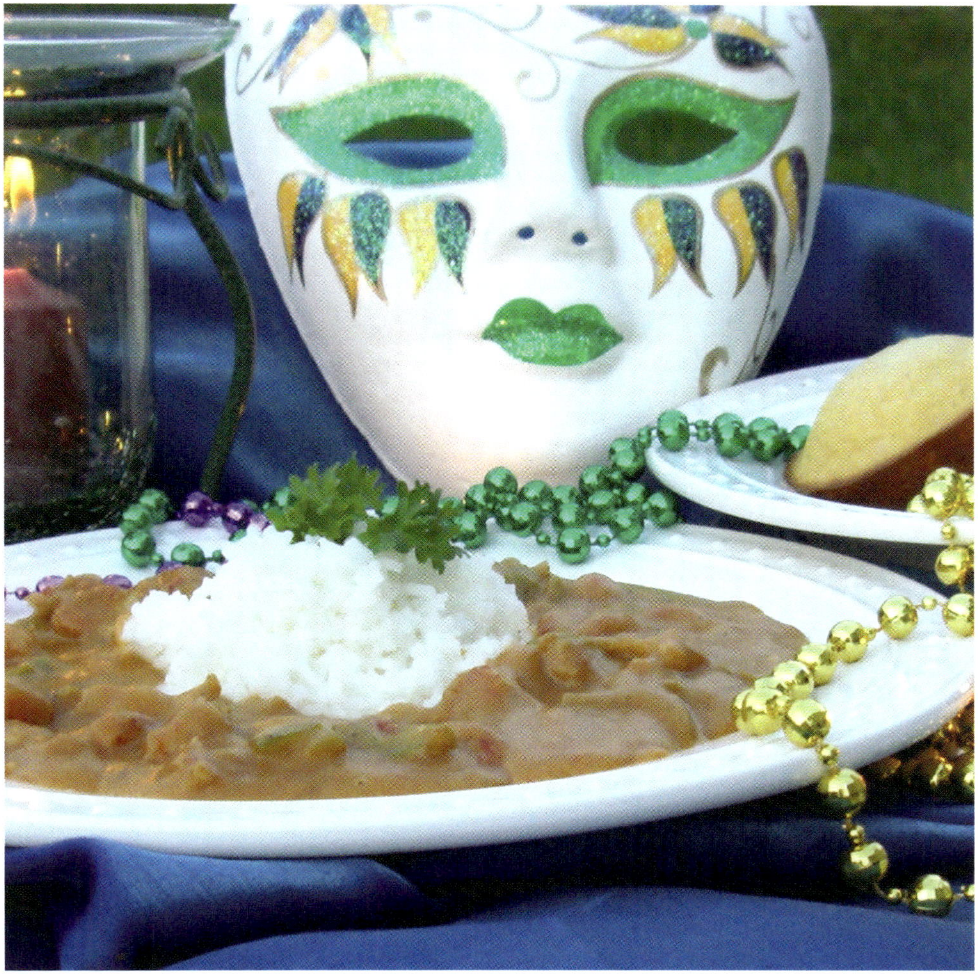

That's right Ladies, eat your heart out -- he's mine!

OH LA LA *Lasagna*

You know, on the off-chance that you are cooking for a lady who may be on the reserved side and hasn't indicated clearly by now how much she appreciates your efforts, I want to tell you that I am really proud of you! You've shown courage, perseverance, love and devotion, all the things that a sane woman could want in a man! And if she doesn't get it by now, don't give up! but *do* consider looking for a sane woman to cook for! But, I am sure she is enchanted with you *and* your efforts. Women are not like fishermen; they don't let a trophy get away, only to brag about it later. You can rest assured you now belong to her!

At this point she will want to show off her trophy! This is when you can expect her to suggest a small dinner party. Remember her friend at work? The conversation they had about the possibility of you 'rubbing off' on Frank? Well here is an old family favorite with a little zip, something that almost everyone loves that should easily feed six to eight people. By the way, I would expect by now, that your lady is starting to show interest in taking an active role in your romantic dinners. Do *not* discourage this. Cooking together is just a way of taking things to the next level. And if you are already there, Bravo!

You can prepare this ahead of time, and then bake when your guests arrive. It gives you time to entertain a bit before you all sit down for dinner.

Menu
Carl's Lasagna
Salad
Garlic Bread

CARL'S *Lasagna*

The Sauce
1- 14 oz can of stewed tomatoes
2- 6 oz cans of tomato paste
36 oz of water
1 tbsp of olive oil
1½ tbsp oregano
1 tsp minced garlic
1 tsp basil leaves
½ tsp each: marjoram, thyme, rosemary, sage
½ tsp "Tony Chachere's Creole Seasoning"
1 Bay leaf

The Meat
1lb ground chuck
1lb ground pork or Italian sausage

The Cheeses
1½ lb shredded mozzarella (you can buy it this way)
½ cup (100%) grated Parmesan cheese
1- 15 oz container of ricotta cheese *mixed with:*
   1 egg, 1 tbsp parsley flakes, 1 tbsp grated Parmesan cheese

The Pasta
9 lasagna noodles

Things you will need
A large skillet or electric frying pan
9x13 cake/lasagna pan
Cookie sheet
A big pot

Brown the ground chuck and the ground pork in a large skillet or electric frying pan. Add the stewed tomatoes, the tomato paste, and the water. Stir until the paste is dissolved. Add the olive oil and all the spices listed for the sauce. Bring to a boil, stirring occasionally. Reduce the heat to low and simmer for 1-1/2 hours, Stirring occasionally. When the sauce is almost ready, put 4 quarts of water on the stove to boil for the noodles. Add I tbsp of oil to the water, it helps keep the noodles from sticking together.

Prepare the ricotta cheese mixture: add the egg, parsley & parmesan. Cover and set aside.

When the water is boiling add the lasagna noodles. Stir carefully so noodles do not stick together or break. Boil uncovered for 10 to 12 minutes. Drain and rinse. It's now time to build the lasagna. Put a little sauce in the bottom of the 9x13 pan. This is so the bottom layer of noodles does not stick to the bottom of the pan during baking. Now lay three lasagna noodles side by side lengthwise over the sauce in the pan. Using a large spoon, spread ½ of the ricotta cheese mixture evenly over the three noodles. It's easier if you use the back of the spoon for spreading the cheese. Next sprinkle 1/3 of the shredded mozzarella over the top of the ricotta, and then spoon meat sauce over the mozzarella to cover. Now repeat the whole process again beginning with the lasagna noodles. Then cover with the three remaining lasagna noodles, the last 1/3 of mozzarella cheese, and the remaining sauce. Lastly, shake Parmesan cheese over the top.

Preheat oven to 350 degrees. Bake lasagna for 45 minutes. (Hint: Place the lasagna pan on the cookie sheet to catch any dripping during baking.) When done baking, place lasagna (cookie sheet and all) in oven and set the timer for 45 minutes. When done baking, remove from oven and let cool for another 35 minutes to firm up.

While the lasagna is cooling, prepare the garlic bread. Butter the slices and then shake some garlic salt on them (be careful not to use too much). Bake in an oven at 400 degrees for about 8 to 12 minutes. You want it to be golden around the edges, but not hard in the center. Finally, cut and serve the lasagna with the salad and garlic bread.

❋ ❋ ❋

Remember Frank? He might feel a bit intimidated. His girlfriend will certainly put the pressure on him. But if he's smart, he will think it over and give you a call about how he can get started on this journey to romance. Remember, "We are all brothers", and in the interest of "world peace" help him out. We men *do* have to stick together. Besides, your worth has gone up in the eyes of your peers, so share the wealth!

By this time, I hope you've figured out that this book is not just a guide to woo a woman into your bedroom. I suppose it could be used in that manner; sooner or later though, she'd figure it out. That would spell the end for you. Not only would she be taking meals elsewhere, but she would put the word out about you and your game.

Rather, it's an attempt to help you transition from being seen by your woman as just another player into a caring, romantic soul that she just can't live without.

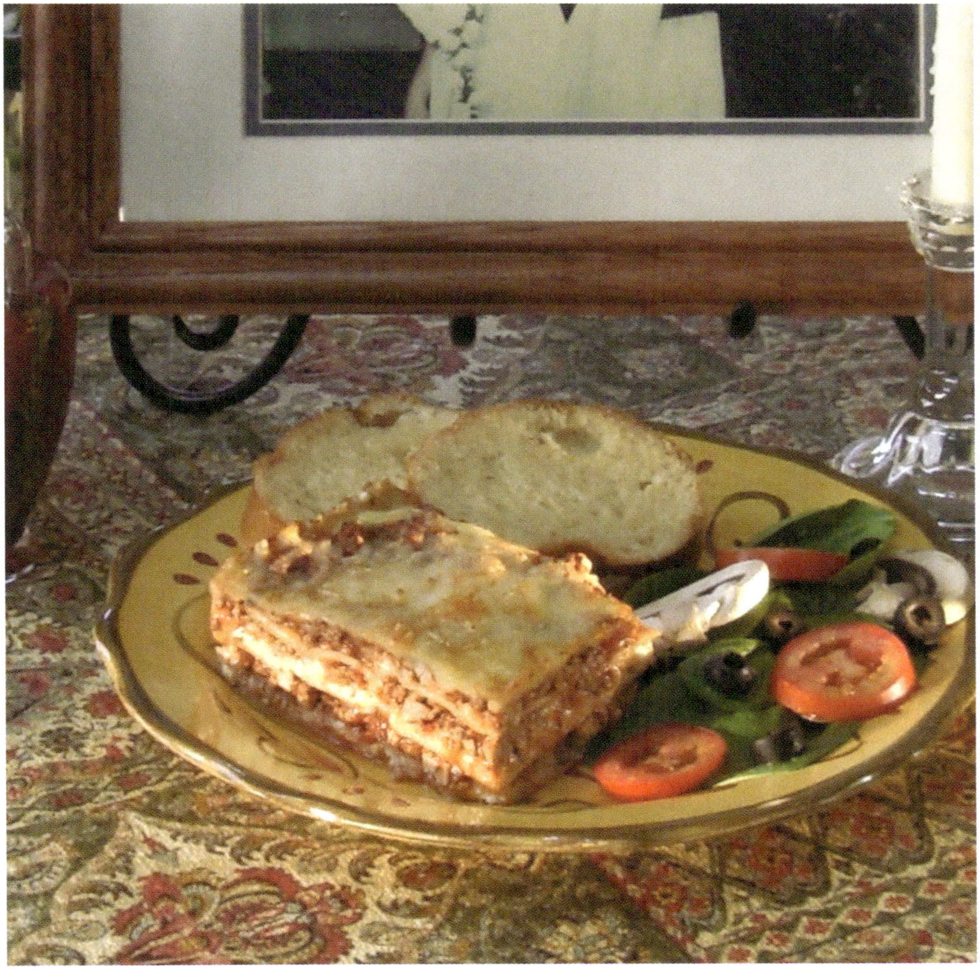

Hmm. This is a refreshing approach!

Notes from the *Range*

You have embarked on a lifestyles and values change that will help you through the bumps in the road as your relationship ages (I know it has for me). There have been times through the years when we've gotten busy and the romance had been misplaced. Invariably my wife would ask, "Where is the romance?" So we would look: It wasn't in the closet. It wasn't in the basement. We'd check in the garage, and it wasn't there either. Where had we last seen it, we wondered? Then we'd remember, it was where we left it last... in the kitchen, patiently waiting to be prepared. Thirty-nine years we've had it. Yes, we've misplaced it a few times in all those years, but I'm proud to say we have always been able to find it again. As long as you keep cooking, the fire should never go out. And the world will be a better place, one romance at a time!

If you have figured that out, then you have just graduated. Congratulations, You now become the teacher, no longer the student. You no longer need anyone else's guidance. As far as the cooking end goes, I hope you have really enjoyed yourself, and will continue! Don't expect to be a master chef, (I know I'm not), but you don't have to be, to make truly good food.

I have included a few more of my favorite recipes for you to try (after all, this *is* a cookbook). Over time, I'm sure you will develop some of your own favorites as well. If you care to share them, please send them to me in care of my publisher, CatsCurious Press (http://www.catscuriouspress.com). Maybe my next book will be 'Favorite Recipes From Romantic Men Around The World!'

Good Luck,

Carl

MORE
COOKING
YOUR
WAY
TO
Romance

SEAFOOD WITH LA SALSA DE *Carlos*

La Salsa de Carlos
¼ cup of olive oil
4 tbsp of butter
2 oz of a white cheese, shredded (We like to use Feta Cheese, crumbled)
½ tsp of oregano
½ tsp of basil
½ tsp of tarragon
½ tsp of minced garlic
½ tsp of caraway seeds
1 cup of milk
1 tbsp of cornstarch (or 2 tbsp of flour)

The Rest
12 oz of seafood (shrimp, scallops, mussels) You can use 12 oz of just one type, or mix as you like
8 oz of linguine pasta
Sprigs of fresh parsley for garnish
Fresh Parmesan cheese to grate

Things you will need
Large frying pan with lid
2 Wooden spoons
Large pot (for cooking the pasta)
Colander (for draining the pasta)
Cheese grater

Fill the large pot about halfway with water. Add a teaspoon of oil. This helps keep the pasta from sticking together. Place on the stove on high heat to boil.

Next melt the butter in the large pan on a low to medium heat, then add the grated white cheese. When the cheese has melted, add the milk, the herbs and the olive oil, but not the cornstarch or seafood. Stir well first, and then add the cornstarch, stirring it in. Simmer for five minutes, stirring occasionally. Add the seafood at this time, cover and keep simmering. You still need to stir occasionally.

When the water in the large pot starts to boil, add the pasta to the water. Stir with a wooden spoon. Boil pasta, checking occasionally to see if pasta is *al dente*. When done, pour into the colander to drain off the water. Divide pasta and place on to plates. Spoon sauce and seafood over pasta, Grate some fresh Parmesan cheese over dish and garnish with the fresh parsley sprigs.

Serve with your favorite salad and bread.

CARL'S PORK DE *La Valle*

The Pork
1 pork tenderloin
1 cup of bread crumbs
½ cup grated Parmesan cheese
1 tbsp chopped Basil leaves
½ tsp garlic powder
1 egg
Olive oil
Dry vermouth

The Financier Sauce
2 tbsp of butter
1 tbsp corn starch
1- 10 ½ oz can of beef consommé' (gelatin added)
6 black olives, thinly sliced
1 can mushrooms, drained
¼ cup of rose or white Zinfandel wine
Salt and pepper to taste
dash of cayenne pepper

Things you will need
A meat hammer with a smooth side
A large frying pan
A small sauce pot
A large glass baking dish

First make the sauce. Melt the butter in the saucepan and add the cornstarch. Blend until smooth. Next add the consommé and simmer on a medium heat until it reaches the consistency of cream. Add the olives, the mushrooms, salt and pepper and the cayenne. Lastly add the wine. Set aside.

Now, mix the breadcrumbs, the basil, the garlic powder, and the Parmesan cheese together. Set aside.

Take the meat hammer and with the smooth side, pound the pork tenderloin flat. Flatten it to about ½ inch. Cut the flattened meat into serving size portions.

Dredge the pork in well-beaten egg, and then in the crumb mixture. Pan fry in olive oil until golden brown on both sides. Place in the glass-baking dish. Pour a little vermouth into the hot pan and capture the remaining crumbs, pour this over the pork.

Pour some of the sauce over the pork and place in a preheated oven on 350 degrees for 30 minutes. Keep the rest of the sauce hot, as you will pour it over the pork just before serving.

CHICKEN *Scaloppini*

The Chicken
2 boneless skinless chicken breasts
½ cup of flour
salt and pepper to taste
¼ cup of olive oil

The Garnish
4 tbsp (1/2 stick) butter
1 onion, thinly sliced
1 can mushrooms (drained)
¼ cup of dry vermouth
1 tbsp of capers

The Sauce
½ tsp of parsley
½ tsp of oregano
½ tsp of dried minced garlic
1- 14.5 oz can of Italian style diced tomatoes

The Rest
8 oz cooked linguine (or pasta of your choice)

Things you will need
A meat hammer
A large zipper-style plastic bag
A small brown paper bag
Two large frying pans (one with a cover)
A blender

Put chicken breasts one at a time into plastic zip-loc bag and pound flat (4 or 5 blows each side). Combine flour salt and pepper in the brown paper bag. Place the flattened chicken breast into the paper bag and shake to coat the chicken with the flour mixture.

Heat the olive oil in the large frying pan with the cover, and place the coated fillets in to brown on both sides. You're looking for a golden brown color. Remove from heat.

In the other frying pan, melt the butter on a medium heat and add the mushroom and onions. Cook until the mushrooms are lightly browned and the onions are transparent. Add the vermouth. Cook a few minutes longer and then ladle on top of the chicken breasts.

Put the remaining ingredients (except the capers) into the blender and blend until smooth. Pour this over the chicken fillets, top with capers, cover and return to a low heat to simmer for about 25 minutes or until chicken is tender, stirring occasionally.

I like to serve this over a bed of cooked linguine.

COQUILLES *St Jacques*
(SCALLOPS WITH TOMATO AND GARLIC)

This dish is not meant as a main course, but makes an impressive first course to a fine dinner such as Spanish Cannelloni.

The Scallops
1 pound of scallops
¼ cup of flour
1½ tbsp of butter

The Sauce
1- 14 oz can of stewed tomatoes
1 tsp of minced garlic
2 tbsp of finely chopped parsley
¼ tsp of salt
Black Pepper to taste

Things you will need
A small brown paper bag
A medium size frying pan
4 half shells (can be purchased at a good kitchen shop)

Put flour into paper bag, then add scallops and shake to coat (dredge). Heat the butter in the frying pan; add scallops and brown for three minutes over a moderately high heat. Add the can of stewed tomatoes, the garlic and the chopped parsley. Season with salt and pepper, stir carefully and simmer over a low heat for ten minutes. Serve very hot on half shells. Use small dishes if you do not have shells.

SPANISH *Cannelloni*

This dish is one of my all time favorites. It's a recipe that takes some time to make, and one that the two of you (I assume by now that she is cooking by your side) can make together.

The Meat Filling
1 lb Lean ground beef
1 lb Ground Italian sausage
2 cups of chicken broth

The Crepes
6 eggs (set out to warm ahead of time)
1½ cup unsifted flour
1½ cup of water

The White Sauce
2 to 2½ cups of milk
3 tbsp grated parmesan cheese
2 oz of mozzarella cheese
½ stick of butter
4 tbsp Flour
Pepper to taste (a couple of shakes)

Things you will need
A large frying pan or an electric frying pan
A medium sized bowl
An 8" Teflon coated frying pan
A medium nonstick saucepot
A wire rack
A roll of wax paper

Brown ground beef and ground Italian sausage together. Add pepper. When meat is browned add chicken broth and simmer on low heat for about 2 hours. If liquid evaporates during simmering, add more. At the end of 2 hours there should be no excess liquid. Set aside to cool.

In a medium bowl, combine eggs, 1½ cup flour, and water. Use an electric mixer to blend until smooth. Let stand for at least 30 minutes. Slowly heat an 8-inch Teflon skillet. Pour in ¼ cup of batter, and rotate skillet around quickly to spread batter evenly. Cook over medium heat until top is dry and edges of crepe start to curl up away from pan. They cook quickly so do not leave them unattended. If bottom of crepes turn brown, then you are cooking them a bit too long or on too high of heat setting. Turn out on wire rack to cool. As crepes cool, stack them using wax paper to separate.

In a medium nonstick saucepot, melt ½ stick of butter and stir in the 4 tbsp flour. Add milk slowly while stirring constantly. When mixture thickens add the 3 tbsp of parmesan cheese and then the 2 oz of mozzarella cut into small pieces. Continue to stir until cheese melts into sauce. Add about 1 cup of this sauce to the meat mixture. Reserve the rest to spoon over the cannelloni just prior to baking.

Assembly
Place 2 tbsp of meat mixture in the center of a crepe, and roll it up. Place filled crepes in individual boat shaped baking dishes, or on oven safe plates, two or three to each dish. (You may freeze the remaining cannelloni to be baked at a later time). Spoon remaining white sauce over the top of each dish of cannelloni, and garnish with a sprinkle of paprika. Bake at 350 degrees F. for 30 minutes.

When done place them on another plate as they will be too hot to place directly on the table. Serve with a salad, your favorite steamed vegetable and French bread.

SPICY CHICKEN (OR SHRIMP) *Salad*

This dish is equally good when made with chicken or shrimp.

The Chicken (or shrimp)
2 boneless skinless chicken breasts or 1 pound of cooked shrimp
3 tbsp of cooking oil
Tony Chachere's Creole seasoning
1 can of mushrooms (stems and pieces), drained
Hard parmesan cheese to grate

The Salad
Lettuce and all your favorite salad ingredients

Things you will need
A large frying pan or a wok
A cheese grater
A bowl

Prepare your salad ahead of time.

Next, if using chicken, cut the breasts into thin strips. Place chicken or shrimp into bowl and coat with Tony Chachere's seasoning. Be careful here, "a little goes a long way" with this spicy seasoning. Put the oil into wok or frying pan, and heat. Add the chicken or shrimp and mushrooms. Fry until chicken becomes golden brown, or shrimp is heated through.

Place some paper towel on a plate and spoon chicken or shrimp mixture onto it to drain off some of the oil. Then top salads with the mixture and add your favorite salad dressing and some grated parmesan cheese.

CHICKEN & BROCCOLI *Pizza*

Bread machine dough
¾ cup of warm water (one minute on high in Microwave)
2 tbsp vegetable oil
2 cups of premium bread flower
½ tsp sugar
½ tsp salt
2 tsps bread machine yeast
"Just follow bread machine instructions for dough"

The toppings
2 chicken breasts, sliced thinly
2 cans of mushrooms (stems and pieces)
1 cup of broccoli (cut into bite-sized chunks)
¼ cup of sliced black olives
12 oz (or so) of shredded Monterey Jack cheese

The sauce
Use the La Salsa de Carlos (minus the tarragon, and caraway seeds)

Things You Will Need
A bread machine
A rolling pin
A large frying pan with lid

Start your dough in the bread machine, and follow all instructions for pizza dough. Next brown the chicken in some olive oil with the basil, and set aside. Then brown the mushrooms in the olive oil and set aside. Chop the broccoli and set aside. Slice the olives and set aside. Make the La Salsa de Carlos (minus the tarragon and caraway seeds). Also do not use the basil as you have already used it when browning the chicken. Simmer the sauce, covered, for about 15 minutes, and then add the chicken. Continue to simmer the sauce for another 15 minutes, then remove it from heat.

When the pizza dough is ready, roll it out with a rolling pin and place it in the pan (I use a pizza pan with holes in the bottom). Let the dough set a half an hour or so, as it will rise some more. Turn the oven to 425 degrees. When the oven has been preheated, spread the sauce with chicken over top of dough. Next add the mushrooms, broccoli, and olives. Lastly top with shredded Monterey Jack cheese. Bake immediately for 25 minutes.

Note: you don't want to add the sauce and toppings to the dough and then let the pizza sit "to bake later" as you will get a soggy crust. The key is to build the pizza and then bake it immediately.

Appendix A

Wine Selection 101
by Dr. John Chamberlin

Does it matter which wine is served with a particular dish? The old rule of thumb was white wines go with fish and chicken, and red wines go with red meats. While this can work well, it ignores the fact that there are today, a very wide variety of both white and red wines, and each has its own set of unique flavors, and aromas.

Good wine has a very complex set of both tastes, and smells. While you don't have to be a wine snob to appreciate this variety, it helps to understand a few of the main characteristics of wines.

White wines are fermented from the juices (but not skins) of wine grapes. Some varieties (like Gewürztraminer) contain very citrus-like sets of both tastes, and aromas. With Sauvignon Blanc, there is usually a distinct aroma of grapefruit, for example. Other, more full bodied whites like Chardonnay, taste "buttery", and have "oak-like" aromas. The aroma comes from fermenting in oak barrels; winemakers control the amount of oak by the length of time the wine spends in the barrel. Other distinct Chardonnay flavors are slight tastes of apple, pear and vanilla. These flavors are not added to the wine – they are characteristics of the Chardonnay grape. The extent to which they can be tasted are influenced by the amount of sunlight the grape received on the vine, the soil and climate in which the grape was grown, and even by the specific type of yeast used in the fermentation process.

Red wines are fermented from both the juice, and the skin of the grape. The skin adds more complex flavors and aromas, as well as tannin. Hence red wines are typically "heavier" and more "full-bodied" than whites. Some red wines contain strong tastes and aromas of berries. For example, most Merlots have a distinct (but light) blackberry taste. Zinfandel has an even strong flavor of berries. The most full bodied red – Cabernet Sauvignon – has strong tannin, or earthy flavors and aromas.

Appendix A

Wine Selection 101 *continued…*

Wine is a complex "spice". When consumed with food, it changes the taste of the food, and the food changes the taste of the wine. Just as a spice is added to a recipe to enhance the flavor of the dish, wine will also alter the taste of the meal. The goal is to alter it in a good way – that is, to enhance both the enjoyment of the food, and the wine itself.

The following are a few simple rules that might help identify appropriate suggestions for a wine to serve with any dish:

1. Drink what you like. If you strongly prefer merlot over anything else, there nothing "wrong" with that.

2. Just as there are "light" and "heavy" foods, there are "light bodied" and "full bodied" wines. Try to achieve balance: serve light bodied wines with lighter foods, and visa versa. Imagine drinking a glass of a very light Chenin Blanc while eating a grilled rib eye steak. The steak would overpower the wine, and would be about all you tasted. Instead, serve a full bodied red wine like a Cabernet Sauvignon – the wine will enhance the taste of the steak, and vice versa.

3. Wines have distinctive flavors. White wines like Sauvignon Blanc have a distinct citrus flavor. Just as the addition of lemon to fish enhances the taste of the fish, the citrus flavor in Sauvignon Blanc enhances the taste of the fish as well. Think of the aromas and flavors in wine as a "spice" or seasoning agent, and match them to foods just as you would the spice or seasoning itself.

4. Start light, and move to fuller. When tasting wine at a winery, you always start with the lighter white wines, and move to more full bodied red wines in a sort of "ladder". If you did that in reverse, the heavy, complex tastes in the full bodied

Appendix A
Wine Selection 101 *continued...*

reds would overpower the subsequent lighter wines, and you would not be able to taste them as well. Apply the same principle if you serve more than one wine at a meal: start light, and move to the heavier, fuller bodied wines later. Many whites go very well with a salad, or bread and cheese, while main courses often benefit from reds.

The following are a few suggestions for wine varietals that might pair well with the recipes in this book.

A. Chicken Parmigiana
1. Sauvignon Blanc. A fairly light, usually fruity white wine. Often tastes somewhat tart, with flavors of grapefruit and lime. Can have a "woody" aroma. Usually good to pair with strong flavored foods, especially with tomato, pepper and garlic sauces.
2. Although the "tradition" is white wines with chicken and/or fish, it doesn't have to be that way. An alternative would be a red Zinfandel, which is a medium red wine, with strong flavors of berry and spice. Zins match well with spicy Italian (tomato and garlic) foods.
3. Chianti is another medium red wine. It is highly acidic, which results in it tasting better with Italian foods than by itself. Chianti has a somewhat "earthy" taste, with fruity flavors and a floral aroma. Because of the acidity, it matches very well with tomato sauces.

B. Grilled Salmon over salad
1. Gewurztraminer is a full bodied, fruity white wine. It tastes slightly spicy, and has a distinct fruity aroma. It pairs very well with fruit, cheese, fish and chicken.
2. Zinfandel. See the notes for Chicken Parmigiana.
3. Pinot Noir is a light, fruity red wine. It often has flavors of cherry, strawberry and other light fruits. It is particularly good with grilled salmon, duck, and dishes with strong earthy flavors (like mushrooms).

Appendix A
Wine Selection 101 *continued…*

C. Tuscan soup
1. Chardonnay is a medium white wine that is probably the most popular in the US. It varies widely among vintners, but usually has a distinct oak flavor, and a taste generally described as "buttery" or "vanilla". Most have flavors of apple, pear and some citrus tastes. Unless it is excessively oaky, it will not overpower most dishes. It also pairs well with bread and cheese courses.
2. Sauvignon Blanc is somewhat lighter than Chardonnay, with a tarter flavor. Usually has a grapefruit or lime aroma. It pairs well with pungent foods, including tomatoes, peppers, garlic, cheeses, etc.
3. Pinot Noir. See notes for Grilled Salmon. Without the sausage in this soup, I'd stick with a white wine. But, the Pinot Noir will pair well with the sausage.

D. Chicken Enchiladas Verde
1. Beer. (I'd go with Corona, for obvious reasons).
2. Gewurztraminer. See discussion above. The fruity and spicy flavors of the gewürztraminer would balance the spicy verde sauce.
3. Zinfandel. Probably not the best match, but it's my favorite wine.

E. Roast duck over rice
1. Pinot noir. See notes for grilled salmon. The danger of pairing something like duck with "bigger" red wines is that the wine can overpower the food. Pinot is a fairly mild red wine.
2. Syrah. This is called Syrah when it's made in Europe or the US, and Shiraz when made in Australia. It's the same wine – a fairly mild, light to medium red wine with spicy fruit
3. Malbec. Malbec is an Argentinean, full bodied red wine. It is somewhere between a merlot, and a Cabernet Sauvignon in characteristics. There is often a detectable plum-like flavor that would go very well with the duck.

Appendix A
Wine Selection 101 *continued…*

F. Crawfish Etouff'ee
1. Gewurztraminer. This spicy dish requires a spicy wine.
2. Syrah. The spicy, cherry, berry and pepper flavors in a syrah would go well with this dish.
3. Zinfandel (the red one, not the white). Again, the rule is to pair spicy wines with spicy dishes. Otherwise, the dish will overpower the taste of the wine.

G. Lasagna
1. Chianti. Chianti is a light bodied Italian wine. It is fairly acidic, and tends to go very well with Italian tomato-based sauces.
2. Sauvignon Blanc. The citrus flavors and acidity of Sauvignon Blanc go well with tomato sauces.
3. Zinfandel (again, the red one). Most Zins are quite flavorful, and have a very detectable berry taste. Again, the idea is to serve a spicy wine with a spicy food.

Appendix B
Setting the Table

Lets start with the dinner plate. Place it center stage, about 2 inches from the edge of the table.

Next to the left of the dinner plate, from closest to the plate out, start with the dinner fork, then the salad fork, and last the napkin. Line the forks and the napkin up on their bottom edge.

Now to the right of the dinner plate, from the plate out, place the knife with the blade facing the plate. Place the spoon next to the knife. Again line the bottom edges up with the utensil on the left. Note: The utensils should be placed about ½" apart on either side of the plate.

Place the salad plate above the forks, just to the left of the dinner plate.

Place a water glass to the right of the dinner plate, just above the knife. Wine glasses should be placed to the right of the water glass lined up on an angle sloping down toward the spoon. If using separate glasses for say, white and red wine. The white wine glass is placed next to the water glass and then the red wine glass on the outside.

If planning to serve desert after your dinner, the desert fork or spoon is placed directly above the dinner plate perpendicular to the other silver ware.

If serving soup, the soup bowl is place centered on top the dinner plate. As soup is eaten before the main course.

If serving coffee, the cup and saucer should be placed to the right of the knife and spoon.

Appendix B
Setting the Table *continued...*

Which glass for which?

Water: A full-bodied glass with a short stem. These will be your largest glasses.

White Wine: A slightly smaller glass with a wide bowl to capture the bouquet.

Red Wine: A wide bowl glass a bit larger than the white wine glass.

Appendix C

Metric conversions
and a few other useful equivalents

Volume
¼ teaspoon (tsp) = 1.25ml
½ teaspoon = 2.5ml
¾ teaspoon = 3.75ml
1 teaspoon = 5ml
1 tablespoon (tbsp) = 15ml
¼ cup (c) = 62.5ml
½ cup = 125ml
¾ cup = 187.5ml
1 cup = 250ml

Weight
1 ounce (oz) = 28.4g
8 ounces = 227.5g
16 ounces = 455g

2 pints = 1 quart
4 quarts = 1 gallon
2 tablespoon of liquid = 1 ounce
1 gill = ½ cup or 2 wine glasses full

1 tablespoon of cornstarch = 2 tablespoons of flour
1 clove of garlic = 1/8 tsp of garlic powder
1 clove of garlic = 1 teaspoon of chopped garlic
1 small onion = 1 tablespoon of dried minced onion
1 small onion = ½ tablespoon of onion powder

In a pinch: sour cream can be made from ¾ cup of milk, ¾ teaspoon of lemon juice, and 1/3 cup of butter

GLOSSARY OF *Terms*

Al dente: cooked just enough to maintain a firm, but not chewy texture.
Bake: To cook by dry heat, usually in an oven
Baste: to moisten meat while cooking with drippings, butter, etc. This adds flavor and helps prevent meat from drying out.
Beat: To smoothen a mixture by vigorously stirring it with a spoon, whisk, etc
Blackened: coated with spices and sautéed quickly over high heat so that the outside chars.
Boil: To heat or bring liquit to the boiling point; to cook food in vigorously bubbling liquid.
Braise: Cooking meat in a liquid that has first been browned in oil or another fat.
Bread: To coat the food with crumbs.
Broil: To cook the food directly under the heat source.
Brown: To heat the meat in oil or butter on both sides, until it has turned brown and become moderately firm.
Caramelize: Browning sugar over a flame, the process of turning sugar into caramel.
Chop: To cut into small pieces.
Clarify: To remove impurities from butter or stock by heating it, then straining it.
Combine: To blend two or more ingredients together into a single mixture.
Crush: To condense a food to it's smallest particles, using a rolling pin or flat sided meat hammer.
Cut-in: To work butter into dry ingredients such as flour.
Dash: A measure approximately equal to 1/16 teaspoon.
Deep fry: To completely submerge food in hot oil.
Deglaze: To add liquid to a pan in which foods have been fried, in order to dissolve the caramelized juices and fat stuck to the bottom of the pan.
Dice: To cut into small cubes.

GLOSSARY OF *Terms* continued...

Dredge: To sprinkle or coat lightly with sugar or flour.
Entrée: This refers to the main dish of the meal.
Fillet: To remove the bones from the meat or fish before cooking.
Fold: To cut and mix lightly with a spoon to keep as much air in the mixture as possible.
Fry: To cook food in hot oil or butter, usually until a crisp brown crust forms.
Garnish: An edible ingredient, like parsley, used to enhance the presentation of an entrée.
Glaze: A liquid that gives an item a shiny surface.
Grate: To shred or cut down a food such as cheese into fine shavings.
Grease: To coat a pan or skillet with a thin layer of butter.
Grill: To cook directly over a heat source, such as charcoal or wood.
Julienne: To cut into long, thin strips.
Marinate: To soak food in aromatic ingredients to tenderize and add flavor.
Mash: To beat or press food to remove lumps and make smooth.
Mince: To chop food into tiny pieces.
Mix: To stir ingredients together until they are thoroughly combined.
Moisten: To add enough liquid to dry ingredients to dampen but not to soak.
Pinch: About a 1/8 teaspoon.
Puree: To blend a food into a thick liquid.
Roast: To cook, uncovered, in the oven.
Roux: A cooked paste usually made from flour or butter, used to thicken sauces.
Sauté: To cook food quickly in a small amount of butter or oil, in a frying pan.
Score: To tenderize meat by making several shallow diagonal cuts across the surface. This also helps the meat absorb better during marinating.
Sear: Sealing in the meat's juices by cooking the outside quickly over a very high heat.

GLOSSARY OF *Terms* continued...

Season: To flavor a dish by adding ingredients such as salt, pepper, or spices.
Set: to let food set after cooking, to solidify.
Shred: To tear or cut food into long narrow strips, either by hand or with a grater.
Simmer: To cooking food in a liquid, such as a sauce, on a very low heat so small bubbles gently break the surface.
Skim: To remove the top layer of fat from sauces, soups and stocks.
Steam: To cook food in a basket over boiling water (but not in it) in a covered pan.
Stir Fry: To fry small pieces of meat and vegetables, quickly, over a very high heat.
Thin: To reduce a sauce's thickness by adding more liquid.
Toss: To thoroughly combine several ingredients by mixing them lightly.
Vinaigrette: Referring to any sauce made with oil, vinegar, and seasoning.
Zest: The thin brightly colored outer part of the rind (or peel) of a citrus fruit.

ABOUT THE *Author*

Carl Wendtland is a man of many talents—builder, woodworker, writer, designer. He has always had a passion for good food but did not begin to cook in earnest until his late twenties. He enjoys the experimentation and creativity that cooking allows and now is the chief cook in his household. He and his lovely wife live in south central Wisconsin in the home they built, where he enjoys building furniture, gardening and tennis. You can contact Carl by using the "Contact Us" link on the CatsCurious Press website: *http://www.catscuriouspress.com*.

Printed in the United States
85754LV00002B